As I Said

A DISSENT

Abby Minor

Published by Ricochet Editions / www.ricocheteditions.com

Cover design by Sandra Rosales

Interior design by Scott Dennison

Cover photograph by Laia Abril, "Ancient Acidic Contraceptives," 2018
Courtesy of the artist © Laia Abril

Grateful acknowledgement is made to Lost Roads Publishers for permission to reprint lines from Frank Stanford's *The Battlefield Where the Moon Says I Love You*. Copyright © 2000 by C.D. Wright, Estate of Frank Stanford. Copyright © 1977 by Frank Stanford. Used with permission. All rights reserved.

Grateful acknowledgement is also made to Catherine Keller for permission to reprint an excerpt from Chapter 1 of *Apocalypse Now and Then: A Feminist Guide to the End of the World* (Beacon Press). Copyright © 1996 by Catherine Keller. Used with permission. All rights reserved.

Ricochet titles are distributed by Small Press Distribution / www.spdbooks.org

This title is also available for purchase directly from the publisher

Library of Congress Cataloging-in-Publication Data
As I Said: A Dissent / Abby Minor
Library of Congress Control Number 2022936820
Minor, Abigail
ISBN-13: 978-1-938900-43-3

FIRST EDITION

in honor—

Marcia Elizabeth Case (1944 – 2016)
exquisite citizen, beloved friend

Ruth Berkowitz (1915 – 2010)
orator

CONTENTS

I

II

III

IV

I

REAL WORDS FOR INSIDE

Something keeps on coming out of nowhere

FRED MOTEN

When it comes to revelation
I myself would prefer to hide it
under a bushel & lay
in the leaf dark (not the new differentdark
but just the under-bushel dark)
where time has hands and windows &
little breezes & the backwater
gas station of my childhood
comes back to me as a purse & I
come back to me as a purse, inaudible
            felt and felt
and folded fold, the god
to put a periphery in. Comes back

to me is—I creep and shout
ahead as I regress—

in the beginning was I went
to a sleepover party at which
the party trick was everyone
tries on the mother's wedding dress & have her
picture taken & go out back
and dare to lick the salt lick. I loved
the salt but not the dress
I didn't want to put it on I cried
and called to go home it was too
big for us we stuck out
the top like tiny dehydrated climbers
on a great, snow-covered mountain.

I cried & called to go home I didn't want
to be a mystery I wanted

            to be funny. I rode home shot-
            gun in my dad's pea-green
            Chevy in the dark in the foot-

hills of the Allegheny Front.

Up in the Allegheny my Uncle Ron says running a flower
nursery will get you the cash you need
to open a superspeedway. My Uncle says
Abigail, complaining about women's rights in America
is like looking at a big shiny serving platter

and seeing one teeny dent. In the seasons, in the valleys, my lover's
father tells me I owe my DNA to the universe. In the foothills,
in the dark, I say I'm a superspeedway giving birth
to a flower shop.

In South Dakota they are looking for neutrinos
underground. Down in a hole
which used to be cracking
out gold I love to lay around
in my white cotton bathrobe w/ pink
roses on it & think about the four known forces
in my purse. Later they feel down

in a hole talking to "the public"
about science & that's how I feel talking
to "the public" about poetry. Yet
people know a lot via April
energies & gas station parking lot
feelings unrecorded, yet a petal
off the dogwood tree is not dark
matter. Do we all understand dark matter.
Something could pass through or we
could pass through it.

What they are about to discover is something
funny that I already know.

I was talking to a young Mormon mowing
the grass at the big country house
where I am the gardener   His wife
is expecting again   We weren't expecting
it to happen again so soon, he said, But
I guess God has
his fingers in everything.

(I am truly not trying to make
fun when I say, Excuse me
Beloved co-worker I totally agree & know
from my own experience
that God's finger
is a dick.)

I would like for a collider
to break me into irreducible components.

I would like Vacation Bible School
to get behind me summer
camps I mean I claim you
I soak you in my corner
I reclaim the Word
I believe in my own Appalachian Jew-
ish dusk. The wandering Jew
is a gawky pinkish plant, each
joint a rooted point, tight white
threads like tent ropes braced. My foremothers'
blood is of no concern to me; born or not
I believe I would have come along
either way, as a paw-
paw or a ghost hand
editing the flyers of evil
anti-abortion adoption
agencies at the public library saying
Pregnant? Scared?

What I have in common with radio Christians
is that we are both obsessed with abortion and we are both uncertain
about the absolute emotional utility of understanding the Big Bang. Or at least
we wish that some of the money used to study neutrinos &

the Big Bang would go to our respective abortion causes. To me
the connections between a vagina and a supernova seem obvious.

If still you see yourself laid
out and are looking
at yourself when
you come as though not making
love as yourself
but as the self making
love to you, don't worry, that's just
the effect of having
the Lord's eyes glued
permanently inside your head.

You can retrain your eyes a little
bit but it's very hard
to do that kind of in-
tellectual work in the nude.
Try to pretend to be
an orange. It doesn't feel
as extra tube-bumpers no
Baby you're an orange but
you don't have to tell anyone about it.
See, I am talking in a citrus way

about a revolution in thought "as great"
            "as the one" "that changed"
"gravity" "from a" "straight-line" "force into"
            "a bend" "in a" "contin" "uum" "and
revealed" "time" "and space" "as siblings"!

If you stepped out one mangy spring
finally rounded, would it be you
triumphant or they? It would depend
on whose eyes you were looking with.

Currently I live in a world where the school board president
comes to the civic club meeting & says we have to rebuild

the gymnasium for like 7 million dollars & then she looks at us
and says, To be honest, I would do anything
to keep my kids off of drugs. Later the civic club VP takes

a drag of his cigarette in the hilly dark and says
To be honest, I used to do drugs in the gym.

I should mention that my father was a particle
physicist. Dipping chew in the darker fields, he approaches

the revelation of a new
    order in which even light
will be known differently. . . Meanwhile, back in the old
    order, as a kid I go for a walk inside

Brookhaven's collider tunnel. The décor
    is underwhelming dirty ivory
computer husks & JCPenney's button-ups, fluorescent
    out in the research trailer swirling
instant coffee, dissolving as the Atlantic
    heaves its brown muscle with mussels
in it, arriving at a roadside seafood shack elided
    under pines. The scientists order beer in green
glass & lemon halves to squeeze over plates of open purple

        clatter, the pines
        make a fragrant column
hung lightly from the sky, up & down it atoms
        smash & shells flash

lines of solder in the dusk. These I take
and clean in the dormitory & wrap secretly
in paper towels, the pretty matter & the heavy

    sea, sand in the roads
    where I unwrap & lay
    my ovate beauty out to be.

I loved your piece on NPR.
I've never been on NPR.
I thought you were on This I Believe?
No, I wasn't.
You seem like someone who could believe.
Thanks.

This poem started out to be about
my first tampon there in the narrow
bathroom air, bathroom shaped
like a train car latticed
with pine light & pine
shadow, where under the sink
my mother's pink
plastic curlers stood erect like space
women in their translucent dome.
Bespoken in my iron finery
pastel pictures round like tiny
portholes showed me how:

In picture 1 you swirl the string
in picture 2 your French-tipped
finger finds its cotton thimble
picture 3 is tampon gliding
home. I'm riding
with a Milky Way now,
stuck up on a chalk stick
secretly along inside & riding
nub-nosed down old
route 220 with my dad in the red
and black Bronco for gas
station chips and chew. So that's
when I knew: All

the green world, all
the brine, I'm just passing
through it, or something's
passing through.

On Mother's Day a guy with a guitar
in a café was looking
for a mom to serenade. I have no children

and I had no children with me
at the time, but he sat down in front of me

and looked at me lovingly. Apologetic (what
could I do?) I said, I'm not a mom. So he left. But still I felt
oracular with little roses at my breast.

Real words for inside are fish-
hook & universe Why
do I have this passage?
—because that's where
under the particular light of place
a lace-work
not recognizably mine. . .
the Big River going by. (Crisis-

filled & stood I am telling
the story I mean
to tell.) For inside I have every
woman in every generation
must look upon herself as if she herself
had come forth out of
Egypt And so on, —

Coming forth
into the garden in milkweed
beds, up-coming iris
have a kind of squeak, up tips
in rain I clip a tip or two
by accident they squeak and fall
this morning into the garden
working here & start to bleed I feel
I am a tulip where I shed my bulb—
I rain some way.

It turns out that yesterday I stood
with my friend and her
belly of baby in a brown lake is part of the story:

the lit brown

smell like warm tea & the fern smell
further out. I wanted
to do a good job of being

the small one, so that we could both

be ferns & perfect
thinking not a lack and not

a burdened body. In lake-
light here is my position:

> *being where my fish marble sits*
> *inside. Not like hers but something*
> *like an abdomen eye, seeing held*
> *in me where we are being held*
> *in tannin-stain, in stain of summer lake—*

It's raining & I know

it must mean something even
if you're not
using it. I know

we could be aperture,
at once seeing
and being ajar.

II

ONCE IN A BLACK SILK GOWN

A FILM NOIR

Ann Lohman, also known as Madame Restell, lived and worked in Manhattan for nearly fifty years. From her arrival in the city in the early 1830s until her death in the late 1870s, Lohman provided abortions, contraceptives, and other reproductive services to those who sought and could afford them. She appears in my view, in my lens, darkened and lit by many forces. These forces, like the soul, are neither separable from nor wholly tethered to the bodies they inhabit.

suppose the camera was in my boat that is slowly drifting away [...]
suppose its reflexes are like those of any of the swift animals in the woods
say a deer for it sees you a long time before you see it
then the machine that made this picture is like a doe in my boat
and I suppose you know how they lift up their heads
and the eyes that are seeing everything the eyes that look through the camera
are those of a spotted fawn so what we see is not what we have ever seen before

FRANK STANFORD, *THE BATTLEFIELD WHERE THE MOON SAYS I LOVE YOU*

The more we rely on nature, and the less we have to do with art, the better.

MADAME RESTELL: AN ACCOUNT OF HER LIFE AND HORRIBLE PRACTICES,
BY AN ANONYMOUS PHYSICIAN OF NEW YORK, 1847

FOOTAGE can break or snap
be lost, or still,

I roll it up
& smoke it, I peer

through a dusty diamond bit:

            I, to be clear, being
lost & still, am a poet camera-

person philosopher archival
vaginal comedian & if anyone

notices any peculiarity
about my nipples, well—

I don't really wonder what *is*
a film noir, I already have 500

,000 pairs of high heels & I'm
a private

eye, myself,
but have you heard

of a floral radiograph? I'd like

to make a feature-
length of x-rayed daffodils, & it

would be a silent film, & the title
cards would go   ONCE

            in a black silk gown, Once
            in a white satin bonnet, Once

in a heavy lace veil—
Once in a private April, Once
she was a clean cord of smoke—

The truth is I was reading, tremble
all over me & one

twilight I found ash on the page,
her horses dark & light

convict me more
than just, *I'm thinking*

about this. She & I
are not the same, but once

I found a black silk gown thumping
softly where it clung

to my heart's red hips. So here

I go—my purple
crocuses are up—I turn books

full of errata to the wall
I clean my eye

I hit record
for about three years I sit

down in my red felt chair because
this is my last chance

to see the wickedest
woman in black &

white who strode the splendid
island by

the sea,
& for a few minutes

the projector just clicks,
a cabbage moth

stutters across the beam.

A PLANT, A DIAMOND, A DARKNESS of the eye. On my silver screen
in my American mind I see salt meadow hay

I see oyster beds

I see the oyster beds
we are always hearing about &

I think there must be a pearl catheter

in the hearts of filmmaking Americans which is kind of like our oyster wound

our inclination to rewind
our anti-greatness valve
our two-way weeping eye.   Here on my screen

I see a different greatness

in me like a pod that's glittery
and dark I see a spark I know
sometimes it makes my whole hand glow. Here

    in my film in a borrowed black silk gown

I make the first scene breezy and low. I use homemade special effects to show purple blossoms on the grass. A pause. Then something moves

within the wetlands, I move my hand under
the blue blanket and it ripples—I'm blazing

with diamonds, I'm driving
in the splendid equipage of my grandmother—

Can I get you a fizzy soda?
Can I ask about your eyes?

Everyone who's watching shivers.
Pouring down the black silk

screen appear an island and two rivers.

HERS wasn't the hand moving under the reeds.
Hers wasn't the hand digging canals.
Hers wasn't the hand writing down names
like *Blommaert's Vly* and possibly having no idea the oysters would expire.

Hers was a later hand
Hers was a deleting hand
Her hands made gentle sparks up and down the city's spine & she was born
as the serving maid Anna Trow. She was born

in England, & cleaned & married & became Ann Sommers, & had a daughter & came to New York & worked as a seamstress, & was widowed, & met the printer Charles Lohman, & together for many decades Ann & Charles Lohman wrote & worked & advertised & freely thought. She was a great writer of letters to the editor & there were two of her I mean she had

two names. She was also

a female hyena / a fiend in human shape / a hag of misery / an infamous
wretch / an audacious woman

of the medium height / possessing / fine proportions / a handsome bust / four
superb horses

purely mercenary motives and / would be considered anywhere / a showy
and attractive woman

—moreover The Most Terrible
Being Ever Born. She was a cleft
& was she accrescent
and on fire? I have these

whistling pink & yellow
flowers here and thinking
in a book about the cervixes

she touched, intelligent

nub-nosed floral episodes
the turpentine or warm-
water spermicides the post-
coital douche. From my kitchen

table with a dozen dark etched &
curetted blossoms standing
in a handmade pot, I tell you:
this is a story about arrangements

of time. In the tinted ceasefire
of the flowerjug I
appear, I move the forsythia
branch here and there among

the cut irises—   April 2nd

in the *New York Times*, "End of a Criminal Life":

Her daughter's daughter: blazing with diamonds, driving in the splendid equipage of her grandmother.

Her house: A fine piece of property, the window shades covered with gandy flowers.

Her body: The right external carotid artery was severed, the jugular veins on both sides were cut through.

In 1878 after midnight on April 1st she
who was known as
the wickedest etcetera got up
in the pre-dawn, filled her tub

with tepid water, unfastened

her nightgown's diamond
button, & opened
her throat with a knife. The *Times*

described her physical body but
they used her symbolic body's
name. Faced with the two which
are one & yet not

the same, maybe I'll call her girl-
friend, me-not-me cosmic
girlfriend of the cord-
grass & of the courts, not

simply flesh & veins but dark intangible
flower that remains. Maybe I'll
run my left hand down
the margins of my paper scraps,

film the phrases
as if they were veils:

> When it snows I
> cast out in the street so
> shiny & we can't
> see her The city
> a treeless mark the
> Avenues were made
> of dust & tea chests
> filled with coal ashes a
> general boom Would all
> the sperm of history
> rise again would all
> the Jersey Meadows skip
>
> as Ladies

wish to be
    who love
their Lords

As a lady
who's a scholar toiled
to write: "Restell

had had enough of rhetoric & withdrew
from the fight." But really it was
Lohman who'd had enough, who turned the bath-
water to salt. Her other
body never had its jugular
veins cut. Yet would I degrade

myself and her &
poetry with the cool
light of reason if
I wrote just to separate
the bodies, to rescue
Ann from Restell—

She chose her name. She wore her heavy lace veil. You have to
understand: It wasn't just that Ann
Lohman performed abortions. It was that, in the 19th century in the
United States, Madame Restell *was* abortion.

I see a body with woodcuts stuck to it
reflected in it, body like a bag
lady made of metal, shiny giantess
and a great conductor. Our Lady
of Conductivity she never begs
to be called good. Like molecules
of silver, lustrous, soft & white, transition
metal thermal and electric how
they pick up images & they reflect

a diamond button, instruments
and trials, solid silver services

and fifty-two windows hung
    with satin—my eye

is hung with satin—behind her
gandy shades, my inner
    inner eye

INTRODUCING George Washington Dixon,

The National Melodist / hustler, circus singer

born in Virginia / jail bird, actor,

writer of meticulous guides

to the city's brothels / journalist &

publisher for the sporting weeklies / forger

fond of hypnotism & commercial sex:

Ann & Charles Lohman hadn't been open for business a year before Dixon started to glue tacky fangs onto Restell in the pages of the *Polyanthos*, making way for all the gluing & etching & forging & tarnishing to come. Not for her the flash swagger, boys will be boys but

Only her fear of pregnancy prevents

a woman from yielding to the sweaty

contamination of a hundred palms.

We shall keep this woman's flag and marrow

bones a crowd to gather whistle "Coal Black Rose"

with the death's head at her mast head until—

In reporting the events leading up to her death, the *Times* described Lohman as "desperate." Incidentally, the Reverend Joel Osteen and his wife Victoria describe the demographic served by proceeds from their greeting card series as "desperate young women." Synonyms for desperate include *frantic, eager, careless, risky, wretched, threatening,* and *determined.* Also *at the end of your tether.* Towards the end of her life

Lohman rambled restlessly about the house. She wrung her hands asking, "What shall I do? What shall I do?" Her agony at times broke forth in moans.

If I sing the body conductive I sing
a singed rail I sing risky, wretched, undivided from
a black silk gown, a white satin
bonnet, a heavy lace veil—

I sing it with my hands
I sing it with my third eye closed
I sing it vaginally,
I sing it zapped and rolling up the dust of the Fifth Avenue.

If I live as a symbolic enemy what
shall I do? What shall I do? Shall I
name my Self for you.

P.S.

Dear Mr. & Mrs. Osteen I thank you for your card.
Dear Mr. & Mrs. Osteen I am desperate please send funds.

ADVERTISED in the New York *Sun*: Female Renovating Pills—An effectual remedy for suppression, irregularity, and all cases where nature does not perform her proper and regular course. They must not be taken during pregnancy, as they would produce abortion.

Revision, March 1839: They must not be taken during p*******y, as they would produce a******n.

Revision, May 1839: They must not be taken during p—y, as they would produce a—n.

Revision, July 1839: They must not be taken during as they would produce.

Revision, November 1839: Safe under all circumstances except one.

From Mme. Restell you could order Portuguese Female Pills for $5/box or $3/half box, while from others you could also buy, For All Disorders Incident to Women,

Ade's White Clover Injection, or

Allen's Mixture, or

Anderson's Vaginal Capsules, or

Apgo Capsules, or

Belcher's Female Cure, or

Blair's Female Tablets, or

Burrough's Antiseptic Liquid, or

Cadet's Injection, or

Carter's Relief for Women, or

Chichester's Diamond Brand Pills, or

Chichester's Pennyroyal Pills, or

Cook's Cotton Root Compound, or

Dr. Cameron's Patent Family Regulator, or

Dr. Caton's Tansy Regulator, or

Dr. Champlin's Red Woman's Relief, or

Dr. Duponco's Golden Periodical Pills for Females, or

Dr. Monroe's French Periodical Pills, or

Dr. Peter's French Renovating Pills, or

Dr. Root's Female Wash, or

Dr. Van Humbert's Female Renovating Pills, or

Dupree's French Specific Pills, or

Edey's Carbolic, or

Farrer's Catholic Pills, or

French Lunar Pills, or

Griffith's Mixture, or

Hardy's Woman's Friend, or

Hooper's Female Pills, or

Lamotte's French Remedy, or

Lyon's Periodical Drops, or

Madame LeRoy's Regulative Pills, or

Mrs. Lydia Pinkham's Vegetable Compound, or

Premo Ergot-Apiol Capsules, or

Rimmel's Medicated Vinegar, or

The Samaritan's Gift for Females, or

Wife's Protector, or

Womanette, or

Velnos' Vegetable Syrup.

Important to Ladies—Especially to those who require an ABSOLUTELY CERTAIN and Speedy Remedy COMPLETE RELIEF—It will cure entirely the worst form of Female Complaints.

Pretty much anything "French"
was for a—n. Maybe

the half box was for if
you were only half p—t.

In spite of brisk competition, it was *her*
conductive body, her lustrous-

ness, that was synonymous
with a—n, so nine times

out of ten you're better
off searching the archives

for "Restellism" than
for anything else.

IRREGULARITY: *Eager*

SUPPRESSION: *Frantic*

PELVIC CONGESTION: *Threatening*

BLOCKAGE: *Wretched*

STOPPAGE: *At the end of your tether*

Return me to my courses   to the dappled track

where mauve and light lie locked   in opposite

the waters   Return me to my enterprise

What one of us does to separate   the waters from

the waters   stars from sun and sea from light

What one of us does with a tansy pill   is done

ONCE in a white   satin bonnet & yes
in a heavy lace
veil & Yes in the heart, where she turns
the most gentle even almost
angelic into the virago

          and shrew: In the tinted ceasefire

of the private, in the heart—I feel a single
pearled bud ovulate in the ceiling
of my heart, it's my iris,
musical darkness, leaves, a sentence
made of lace & lesser fire, when I read

in a very old newspaper a
  gentleman saying it's
          In the heart
of *this* Metropolis she holds
Her bloody empire.

In the heart of this metropolis George
Washington Dixon once

had a body   also
his symbolic body
was Zip Coon   Dixon created

this symbolic black body
          to express fantasies &
fears—A Glorious Collection of Nerve
Working, Side Cracking, Care Destroying

SONGS—but did his symbolic black body
have a (symbolic) (white) penis   In his very snug striped trousers

at the Bowery Theatre

singing *Lubly Rosa, Sambo cum*
Don't you hear de banjo tum, tum, tum! And in fact

here's an oyster connection: His rivals couldn't decide whether
Dixon was mulatto or white, and so when he went to prison
for libel a pissed-off upper-class enemy wrote He is now caged

and we may hope
when he comes out will go
to opening oysters
or some other employment

appropriate to his color.   But instead

he opened papers   covered trials
published a woodcut

print of Her—was it she or *she*, whose
dark collar, whose hatched cheek
rising above a winged devil gum-deep
in an alabaster baby with adorable
little fangs? He sang   *'Cause you're dark*
don't start a' pinin'

You're a cloud with silver lining   So

What's going on with Zip Coon? What's going on with Madame Restell? What's going on in the theatre, at the prizefights, in the brothels, in the pages of the sporting weeklies, where you can read about the felons of today & yesteryear? For pennies a young clerk could buy papers such as Dixon's *Polyanthos*, devoted to Popular Tales, Anecdotes, Poetry, Satire, Humour, Sporting, and the Drama.

Because I too am devoted to poetry, humor and the drama,

I step into the ring I say Young clerks, brothers,
brothel-goers, minstrel-lovers—I ask you:

Does grief   attend the sporting man? Exclaim

a thousand voices: Let us have
Zip Coon! to apprehend
our bawdies beneath a black veil,
and with a black veil let us bind up

the body of Madame Restell.   So bodied, the sporting man

will have his license. The black dandy be
his hansom, and the white woman fiend
his paving stones. As for "Coal Black Rose," he whistles—

he suckles—he sings electric
on the American stage. He studies
the stain & the sweat.   Sporting men, I ask you:

Whose stain?   Whose sweat?
Whose palms?   Whose fiend? Whose loins, upon
whose loins?

A CLOSE-UP of Three Cast-Iron Tubs:

ANN LOHMAN'S TUB, in the very Air where once bright Glaciers moved—on the second floor of her last and largest house at 52nd Street & 5th Avenue—Inclosed by a light wood work with folding doors, chemise and night-dress thrown over a chair—which could at any moment become dangerously decorative—A wood work Incloses glacial underclothes—Underlain with schist, in the very Place where once great Tulip trees & purple meadow Parsnips grew—Where moon & sunlit orchids moved, glow her curious underclothes.

THE POET'S TUB, painted sage green with two spray cans from the hardware store—Bought for a hundred bucks out of a front yard where it had served as a pansy planter—interior enamel flakes off when filled—Down the drain have gone sperms, hair, vetiver soap, boiled dye for making bride's maid dress, menstrual blood, rose shampoo—Poet has been warned by contractor friend that sliding around in the bath could result in an enamel-chip-infected ass cheek, & same friend said when poet raised the subject of this work, "I never would have thought that about you."

THE POET'S CHILDHOOD TUB, upstairs in a threadbare farmhouse crammed into the foothills of the Allegheny Front—four claws planted in rust-red shag—In which she often lay wearing all of her mother's Rings and asked to be called Pearl—& had a fascination with the drain—Why so whirlpool, why so dark—Underneath the sink, pink hot rollers like spacewomen stand ready in their own clear plastic ship—They heat up—To be the best kind of woman, outer space or undersea.

INTRODUCING a Physician of New York, a student
of nature / a calm & philosophical observer /
anonymous author of *Madame Restell: An Account
of Her Life and Horrible Practices*, 12 ½ Cents
and Sold by all dealers in Cheap Books:

Maternity Is, and Should Be, the pride and glory of the married female.

No woman has the right to Tamper with her own Constitution.

I hope you will understand
these men I introduce
to you as tedious scenery, & now more brightly
upon the screen appear

two rivers pouring forth from two
celestial tubs:
from the west comes laughing
fast the River Is, & see

my hand writing down the east
in spindly old mappish
red, the River Should Be.
The rivers Is and Should Be

border me, estuary me, make of me
an archipelago; I feed
kettle ponds which is
& should be kettle ponds

between them. In my oaks
palegreen orchids grow
which are & should
be flowers; flashing in

the river waters, silver-
sides which are
    & should be fish. Dear
Student of Nature,

Dear Sir: The River Is alone
moves one-and-a-half
million metric tons of
sediment—ochre, silver,

sable, gloom, & straw—
with every loop around
the sun. The cosmic black & best
laid sands. You wouldn't need

    to say I
should be
    it, if I am.

So yes anonymous elucidator
of Constitutions, I am
the great Tamperer—I fiddle
with my formation—I tweak

my creation—I mediate
my shape. I've even written
    a new anthem
for the nation; please rise:

Her creation to snoop, the

bombs bursting in air—how
so charter to rig   her
the form was still there—

Considering *is*: you're just bewildered and mistook.

Considering *should be*: you're just wicked and you suck.

Considering *myself*: I'd rather suck than be mistook & such
is the subject of this book—

That she was again and again called bloody as though
it wasn't precisely blood
that her clients were looking for.

AT THE IDEA of her being
a female hyena, I splash
around & leap
from the tub. I flap

my Pearly tail & float
forth into the Jersey Meadow
dusk. Between two
rivers, my laughing lupine

girlfriend barks & I
sing back, we meet
& play the lupanar
game We set up rugs

& rocking chairs
among the rushes
& the reeds.

This film proceeds

along the logic of a bouquet, cut things
rough & delicate, accrescent
& cleft, visions & events all
gathered together in a single fist. Like molecules
this film proceeds, there's a strand of amber-
colored leaves dead in the diamonds
of a chain link fence, on Blackwell's Island roughly
in the place where the gothic

penitentiary once stood. Looking across the East
River at Manhattan, I record maybe ten thousand
windows, & brickwork, sumac rooted in the sea-
    wall, & the claws of Queen

Anne's lace. When she spent one
pesky year in the middle
of the river, in the middle of her career, some
accounts suggest she lived, as other infamous
& powerful prisoners did, in a cell always
unlocked. Her husband came &
went as he wished while the poor
and mentally-ill prisoners built the sea-
wall, quarried the black stone where
I sit and watch one black
    brant flash, & fish—

A CLOSE UP of Nineteen Facts vis-à-vis the Life of Ann Lohman, *alias* Madame Restell— HER SECRET LIFE-HISTORY—Full Details—Who her Victims were, and how she held them in her Power—Her Tricks and Devices—SHOWING HOW SHE BECAME RICH—What She Did and How She Did—ALL ABOUT HER—

Her head is well formed

Her hair is admirably arranged

Her exquisite gold buttons

Her figures of bronze

Her one major imprisonment

Her two major trials

And the April 1st trial
she didn't show up for

I unfold her black silk gown

and make of it a living black silk doe

her white tail flicking free

and her river stone nose to the grass

I have seen the wicked flourish

like a green bay tree, begins

a rather unflattering book

published shortly after her death

Although her figures of bronze & spacious parlors were certainly noted, it was her solid silver dining services around which so many unfriendly observers whimpered and slunk. Incidentally, what most obsessed the House Select Investigative Panel on Infant Lives when they interviewed Planned Parenthood President Cecile Richards early in the 21st century was her salary.

No bootstrap love, no baron approbation.

Then there was the eminent gynecologist saying, Shall the West and South be filled by our own children or by those of aliens? This is a question our women must answer; upon their loins depends the future destiny of the nation.

Laws were changing

piece by piece

Women traveled from out of city and out of state

That's why it's an action film

Not the detestable old French hag that some imagine her to be

Some doctors argued that withdrawal led to insanity

On the other hand there were the Sex Radicals, the Free Lovers, the ones who advised that a wool ball stuck as far up as possible should be as much a part of a woman's evening costume as her nightgown.

If I sing her Tricks & Devices I sing
a wool ball, I sing one of the prettiest
women in the room, *The Lady*
in Black, the organs

of union, let them
be magnetic—

A STAR has fallen. That's what Dixon wrote to announce a new prostitute in town.

WATER'S a connection
I'd like to make, how
for millennia many
people considered menstruation

water's twin, how the pecuniary
Dutch drained Manhattan
saying If water hurts you
you may turn it away. Now on a rail-

road trestle above the green-
gold creek in my own summer
backwater, I step over
snakes asleep in the

herbal sun. I go
down to the bank
& swim. Now hologram-
textured Olmsted's

beside me, Central
Park's architect saying Mere
rivulets are uninteresting.
Water's sparkling down

my legs. As she dunks
sheets in vinegar So many hands
make the kills & creeks go
here & there, fill in under-

water & send water
under land. These
gentlemen had no
essential interest in

unrestricted flow. I raise
my arms up to the splendid
sun and go, Excuse me,
          sirs: this is H_2O.

INTRODUCING Anthony Comstock, Confiscator

of obscene materials / eradicator of vice / enemy of infidels and free lovers, who you may know from his work as a Special Agent of the U.S.P.S.—

There's a hymn that goes So often I'm surrounded with enemies from Hell & for her that was Anthony Comstock. And so she withdrew. Dear Anthony I'm taking you down off the shelf I'm undressing you. You're dusty. Here's one thing we have in common: When I was a soldier in the Civil War & the other guys set my room on fire cause

> I was such a teetotaler, I tipped my whiskey ration on their cocks. Cocks
> afire. I confiscated their cocks. Dear Anthony you better
> come over to my house right now. I impound you I force you
> to play poetry games. So many people

have disliked Anthony Comstock. In retrospect it's true the federal law passed in his name created problems for a lot of us. It wasn't until 1971 that Americans were once again allowed to send information on contraception through the mail. Or until the next year that the Supreme Court got around to striking down state laws prohibiting the use of contraceptives by unmarried persons.

> Have you ever seen the kind of porn that Comstock confiscated?
> A single hand-drawn cock stands up among ruffles
> and britches in a bucolic scene, a fine lady about to sit down upon it.

Comstock and other members of the New York Society for the Suppression of Vice were upset about Race Suicide, white lady's killing all the children she's not having. Not only killing the not-haved children but killing some larger concept which is somehow herself because it is suicide. Very many people in America still worry about this on their websites.

> Anthony, I'm on a taskforce all about
> how to deal with you. Let's confiscate everything:

trashcans, apartments, seed pearl, underclothes,
liquor, diesel, tune books. Let's make a pile of the world
and sit on it. Then very slowly one by one let's
put everything back.

"Death is a lie" I heard a voice
sing on the Christian radio and I thought
Great news, this is great.

VOICE, OVER: Very quiet [2018]
gray-blue white light
sadness. Then a variation of palest rose
in the sky. Echo of April
again, ache of spring, a city street
glossed with sun, the ochre
crabapple buds, trains
moving off into the distance on trellises in variation
of rose light. Is it my sorrow that this is coming

to an end? I want something
very plain & very
common to be true: that when you have

one name you always

have two. Drifting away
from your name
is a shoreline, it is neither the garland
of jasmine nor a necklace
made of skulls.

(No music): Show her hand
sweeping eraser dust
from a page. Show her
horses dark & light her
weaving cinder &
plum. Her cool light
of reason her ergot &
turpentine powders her
letters to the editor, her
Voice:

I cannot conceive how men who are husbands, brothers, or fathers can give utterance to an idea so intrinsically base and infamous, that their wives, their sisters or their daughters, want but the opportunity and 'facility' to be vicious, and if they are not so, it is not from an innate principle of virtue, but from fear. What is female virtue, then, a mere thing of circumstance and occasion?

It's here with much
   blue milky
wallpaper with the whitish pattern raised

to the touch, here within my dry township
within the illusion of the future
as suture that I write—pomegranate
seeds, kundums, cohosh, a general
boom in her left hand history
isn't but my nipples could be
            The End—

(No music, February 1878): Comstock came posing
as a customer she asked him
to come back & sold him a box
of pills he produced
a warrant for her arrest she invited
him to ride with her
in her carriage down
to the station & so together rode & so
we sway together like fleas in the long
feathers of her hat held
from the inside we
together ride.

SPIRIT I am alone & am I
alone and filled with saints
to navigate her bodies? Once

in a black silk gown Once in the muddled
teal of mid-Atlantic dusk. Reader,
my reader: pin back your ears. It's

the hush of mantilla lace it's
the sound of her horses rolling
up the dust. Once

I was a clean lace of smoke.
Very strange things happened in the court.

SIX SCENES OF TRIAL [1847]

Tiny transcripts printed
by the thousands & sold
on cheap paper Showing

        to Females the Perils and Terrors Of an Invasion of the Course of Nature

A Warning Lesson to Females who Err: "WONDERFUL TRIAL"
Third Edition—Price 6 ¼ cents. Sold by Wholesale & Retail

Agents in New York City, Philadelphia, Baltimore, Albany,
        Troy, Boston, Hartford, New Haven,
Providence, Utica, Rochester, Auburn,
        Buffalo, Cincinnati, Louisville, Vicksburg,
                New Orleans, Mobile, Richmond, & Washington, sold

on silk & on fire, a treasury
of funny Terrors &
Perils, a warning, a Warning
        Lesson yet—

I.
Witness.—On Tuesday I
asked her to let me
  see what came
from me; I merely
wanted to see how
it looked. She set it
behind the fireboard
  in the room
where I was; it was
between daylight
and sunrise.

D.A.—It is for you as jurors, fathers, husbands, and

brothers to say—At what time did the intercourse commence? Did you notice any peculiarity about your nipples? What else did you find or feel?

Witness.—A dark streak
came around them.
Madame Restell
admitted me at
  the door.

> The defense claimed that Maria
> Bodine had never been
> pregnant at all & so the jury
> asked for more information about
>
> the appearance of a pregnant
> person's nipples. They requested it
> thrice. The majority of us,
> they said, Wish for it.

II.

The Defense.—I believe that woman and Christianity are the only things that keep men from devouring each other like wolves but Maria, when do you say was the last time you had intercourse with Cook?

About the middle
of May I did not
tell that I had been
  out of, or lost
my courses I did not
tell that I had lost
them and gone
to New York to an
old lady who

had relieved me
  I did not say
so, nor
anything like it.

Q. In what situation did you then discover yourself—*A.* No sir, I did not. We did not speak very loud. Q. Where is Madame Restell's house, and how did you discover it—*A.* I think she locked the door. Q. What else did you find or feel—*A.* I found

a curtain I lay
down as directed and
  for five or ten
minutes she made
an examination
with her hand
she inserted
  her hand
up my body,

In what part of your body?

(In a whisper, but
audible, and
repeated by
the D.A.):
In the vagina.

> The defense then proceeded
> to show the manner in which
> the character of man and
> that of woman is formed.

III.
Witness.—I left her
house for the boat but
  a short distance I
remained from Greenwich
street to the foot of
Duane; I think on
Tuesday in bed all
  day I had taken no
medicine but
laudanum to ease
  my pains when I
arrived I went to
bed but a few minutes
after I rose the next
morning to attend
to my household
duties, I was obliged
  as a serving
maid Mr. Cook went
with me at the starting but
  I was alone.

Persuaded to sign a complaint, barely
above a whisper, having just that
morning been examined by a doctor
who reported that the neck of her

uterus was indurated & excited & that
the excitement was not solely
produced by his finger; blushing &
hesitant, weeping & simpering, Maria told:

I had cold
  chills on me

I never left the
room she fixed
the bed and
  assisted
me in, I expressed
no wish to leave
it, I did not want
  to quit it—

What did you say to her, or she to you?

She took thirty
dollars she
slept with me.

IV.
A Doctor.—In my opinion, the mere introduction of the hand
into the vagina would produce in

a nervous, sensitive, excitable, or even ordinary temperament
hysterics, convulsions, it might be,

death. Really I ask any gentleman of common sense to decide
upon that question it does not

require a doctor.

V.

Q. Supposing the hand were introduced and worked round and round, so, what would be the effects? *A.* The most horrible. Q. Could a wire be under the finger at the time of such an operation? *A.* Undoubtedly, that's the way the thing is done. (Great sensation throughout the court.) Q. Doctor, at what period in gestation does a woman's size begin to alter? We are all groping in the dark. *A.* Very soon after pregnancy. Some females will have the appearance as early as three months. It depends upon the make. Q. At what period does the rotundity of the figure increase, so as to require a female to unhook her dress? *A.* That does not fall exactly under my department.

VI.

It's difficult to find out what
Maria Bodine wanted or how
she felt because the woman
never wrote poems. Maybe

she loved sex or never wanted
an abortion at all or maybe
she didn't want to be sleeping
with her boss. In the transcript:

Yes, Madame said
she would rather not
  give me
an abortion and I
had better come
and stay and board
the time out. I said
  I was six
months gone and
would rather stay
and board the
time out at $5
a week but my
  beau would object
to the charge. So

there goes Maria sent down
the Hudson to be put right, so back

& forth for money, so saying
of her breasts, I must wrap them

in red flannel and
  rub and draw
them out with a smoking
pipe. Twice I
  hallooed out
a glass of water
and a light I suffered $75
and no less my breasts
pained me very
  much and milk
came from them over
my dress Spirit
  who are lee who are green
Hudson still sprigged I
  engrave I look I took
a great flooding there.

Aftercare back in Ramapo from
regulars who thought Maria had
disease of the spine was non-
stop cupping & leaching for six

months. Bodine's lawyers called
Lohman the most terrible
being ever born & Lohman's
lawyers called Bodine as foul,

corrupt, loathsome, guilty a
thing as ever polluted God's
blessed earth by her pestilential
presence. The beau/boss Mr.

Cook was never called
to court & in all the talk
of Bodine's ill-health anemia
never came up. Many things

never came up. Many things
remained beneath. Lohman
never spoke, her mouth
was described as an iron

line, but her head was
round & round
the iris of my camera
I plait forsythia, I plait

crocuses, I stand ankle-
deep in the earth where
flowers grow as I approach
the last day, the last

of nineteen days, on the last
day was the first time
a deer came up,
an Indian came up, but they

remain in the dark, un-
recovered: three hundred
white men filled
the court, their words

filled the court, their words
weirdly sublime & cornered by

lack of magic:

The Defense.—An Indian sold a deer, which he represented as being in a boat on a stream far distant—how you were to go through a field, then through a wood. He was corroborated in every particular except the deer. So in this case. Maria Bodine is corroborated in going into the defendant's house, in coming out, but as the Indian did in the other case, in the abortion she fails.

Yet the jurors swerved not
from their duty the counsel
did not quail and that very
female elaborately trimmed
up for a witness turned out
the veriest harlot the foulest
trull that infests our streets or
emerges from the perlieus of
the Points draggles her dank
wet skirts through the mud
on a rainy night & "Caroline

Lohman"—they got her first name
wrong—"alias Madame Restell,
stand up."

ONCE I the poet took a bath about a hundred
and thirty eight years after

the Madame's death, in May, in the hot
smell of diamonds I lay thinking this

is a story about arrangements
of time. In the tinted ceasefire

I greet every cervix & all
the sperm of history & reader,

my reader: pin back your ears.
It's the hush of mantilla lace it's

the sound of my neighbors burning
milk jugs in the yard. To the window I turn

my eyes & see my own
underwear at the moment blowing

off the line across
the lawn like cotton shopping

bags as Ladies
wish to be, I see most

            clearly as a big woman
in the *National Police Gazette*

she looks chivalrous engraved
as a flying fat-faced devil spreads

its brunet wings in 1847 spars
an itsy ivory baby that doesn't look

too different from paintings of
the Madonna to me.

LEAVING THE NEW YORK HISTORICAL Society Library, this
is a quiet scene. That's me, in a red hillbilly sweater, I cross

into the trees and snow thinking

microfilm! Whoa. How
dental. Not only the click, and the color, and the medical
smell, but like x-rays of the mouths of men
who created
and hated her, so many chipped & oily

words lined up in rows, black husks
of sunflower seeds stuck

in their old teeth.   Going into Central Park now I freeze

away all unworkable grief & go
into the nourishment of black
ice, white, deep green & smoke. I loved going in

to the reading room, I loved the heavy sage
green drapes, twenty feet high & tied
with gold cord. I loved wearing a name tag, & no
pens, and only five sheets of paper
allowed, feeling so dreamy
every time I pushed the ponderous
door the wrong way. The whole time I was

          peering into something murky, a huge

black diamond on the screen. One tract
about her warned
women who might
abort: Write this
in letters of fire on your memory.

And have I? And have I
yet? And have I written
a burn upon my secret brain? My memory
is aflame.

What I needed   wasn't there
in the archive, but rather at the angel

of Bethesda, her wings
upswept, cast
like sharp semi-colons against
the sky. And the people—my people—going carefully

across the terrace, across the bright red fishbone
pattern of frozen brickwork underneath.

                Was I
an angel? Was I
a fiend? Was I infamous, &
luminous? I saw you there,
people, cold to the bone, taking
pictures of yourselves with the angel in her bare feet,
with a bronze lily
in her left hand. I saw the lake
like a thin black diamond
in the bezel of the red emergency
ice rescue ladders, oddly delicate, hung
on hooks at intervals along the shore.

In one court transcript it was written,
        THE PEOPLE
        VS. RESTELL,
        alias LOHMAN.

And in the park, above the angel, I saw two
        equivalent geese

in the sky.

I have humility before gowns
made of metal. I have humility
before veils, before the waters, and the ratchety
glass eye.   No dead man will catch me stooping

to prove that she was *good*. I am not waiting
for fabric made of bronze, no matter
how lifelike, to flutter
open. I'm just standing out here
with the people vs.
an empty fountain. The people
vs. two geese in the sky. The people
blazing with diamonds, riding, perhaps, in the splendid
equipage of our grandmothers, trailing
their long sentences, their
long letters of fire. And still my camera
rolling, wondering—

Is heaven
a city? Is the apparition of her, the veil of her,
a city, or a garden
within a city? I don't know,
after years, what she is, what heaven
is, what the island is with
its birds rising like handfuls of chipped porcelain
and smoke. On Blackwell's, now Roosevelt, the most beautiful gull
landed beside me, we were both
hunting
by the river, & her slender black
beak was like a pen or a curved
barrette. Together we sang
a little song & it went, I have always felt
accompanied beneath the river veils, &
the veils of stone, by

nothing, by
nothing at the bone.

And do I, will I ever suffer such
obedience, not to beg
to be called good? Once

in a black silk gown.
Once in a white satin
bonnet. Once in a heavy

lace veil. Pollen, Ann, a semi-
colon, an iris, a silver some-
thing other than *Or*—

If I were only Chaos why
would I wear these jewels?

III

BLOOD DRESS
A DIARY

This is your defect
it might as well be
a diamond.

ALICE NOTLEY

ᘐ

Beneath codeine, sunflowers burn. So I can hear

the immensity of rains, *We are a sea.* So I do not believe
that we are not "in" heaven; the white summer blanket, the being, the coming to be.

Once my father walked me through the full moon of a particle
        accelerator before it was activated. Once I heard that the womb
is lemon-sized. Because of the rose my mother planted
outside my father's death-room window, because of the photograph I keep
above the bed of Georgia O'Keeffe's hand and breasts, I have never felt alone
        with all these particles here, these tattered buds
smashing in the dark.

        They gave me a blue plastic glove and a number to call
        if passing blood clots larger than a lemon. Then in the light of my prehistory

I washed a few galaxies of roses from strips of cotton cut from my lover's shirt.

ᘐ

In the fields yet to be quarried for stone ,   lovingly spent
        all morning cutting out colors
and gluing each letter down. Sometimes a rainy fear still falls in me, I mean falls
in a way that's still.

Yet I've been created in the image of a great storm drain—

I wash ,   I accede
what down pours. Moving towards

the collective waters, I've drifted further than that lace-light shimmering
like a papercut on the wall. I'd still like to tell it now but *I*
        is someone else.

On a single water *I* is an interview

most heavenized.   These were my last words:
                                                                        "A small glass, an apple tree
in bloom, to be left alone
                                                among these things." And then I changed; I fell down

through every air; two women stood on the other
        side of a chain-link fence, their hair and skin
the color of sweat-stained linen. Their dark book
        in their hands. "It's a sad day," one said.
For a moment   I didn't even realize who they were.

I can't tell whether I've been left out or have wandered off,
        just that in the dream of a powerful sun

there was a trick of looking at something else first to protect your eyes.
Someone showed me how to do this from the deck of a ship, to behold

pitch glitter and gold, concentric ripples and rings.   Unfolding

        these patterns ,   here are the rags stained
and stained now ,   colors of bark burned

        into cotton, this annealing, becoming more
bark-like in its lands. Once I found tiny crayons

wedged in pregnant Barbie's pop-off stomach
with a set of plastic shoes.   The man with bleached coyote teeth
and coon dicks at the flea market said, "I sell more of this stuff to girls
        than anyone else."

In the last few hours of my twenty-eighth year, rain fills the backwater
summer night with patterns, jade patterns, black patterns most

clean and old. Coursing down to the corridor of cinder-
block strip clubs along the Susquehanna River, driving southeast at dawn. To arrive

in the walking place , where my heart

surrounds the building while we watch Food Network with the blinds
closed. Never to forget the others, with whom I wanted so much
to speak. To say, *Stand to me*

my nations in the dark— to cross, to cross

the borders towards the orchard fire ,

years ago

I walked across a room and knelt

by the couch where he slept. His rainy eyelashes un-rained the light. Woke up smiling
and said, "You're wearing a dress." I've never cared to write

about sex, though I've been floating
away from the sun, down to the sea. Towards egrets white enough to write on

in the shallows. Somebody testing urine, testing blood. River grass
glimpsed from the road. Towards four white tablets, glowing there

in the circumference of the summer like four teeth, four unstylish buttons, four drops of milk, four O's. With the moon up

to my left and the sun going down to my right, blazing opal and yellow
clock fire. Into myself four tablets one at a time,

at the same time. Into myself the lace-light, not backlit
but dapple. Like I was a woodblock printed
perfectly
yet different onto paper.

The paper uterus taped to my yard sign was an attempt to reconcile
a feminist-anarchic-folk aesthetic with the less subtle
realities of nationhood. There are very few situations

in which floating down the Mississippi by yourself actually works.
Once I saw a fawn alone on the path
and I thought she was a little flame; I believe I am now formed
as tiniest silver seeds.

The worst thing
was how they torched the continent of our bodies,
made us afraid to return. The Congressman's aide in black spikes

with charms dangling off the heels said, "I think we've had a productive discussion."

The world changes from rinsed mist to gray fire   and how pridefully

still I carry my overcries: One

is the color of rooibos shot through with minnows.

One is iron cerulean from when a stranger's voice came inside.

One is gutter-colored, ache from reading, "Not wanting

to tell, she locked herself in a bathroom and quietly bled to death."

These colors live together all in one place, this place which has eyes,

the eyes of the white-tail doe. Gaze of water waiting

        to cross to water.
        Who will bring me

to my boldness? After all these centuries, I stand by the genital mysteries.

Now I see a bug with wings the color of a tiger. In darkness

        in the gold of darkness
        a bit of candle opens up the paper-
        cut between seconds.

Appalachian pre-dawn so arriving heat of blue so I choose a long ,   loose
        black skirt patterned

with the white silhouettes of glass bottles of perfume. Because I would like to be clear,
and cleared, transparent, a form of love :   If I were a polymer sheet I would lay down

upon the details to flatten, pin, and brighten them; in the end
        all I intended was to describe July's
        etched, over-etched green. Sometimes I get haunted

by the wound of explanation, and the wound of getting along. I went into a sadness
after I told my "story" for the tape recorder, why hadn't I talked about my beloved's
        eyelashes, person who's a bay

in which I drift, and the long plank of his chest (upon which
I talk and weep and laugh and rest)—and the Norway maples, the un-metaphorical

        hoof beats in the street, just the basics, how the moon is held
        like a small gold jewel in the bezel of a tree? Never really knew what to do

with the details, with the pale blue + sign, with the mill race water, with two-
lane roads drifting through the valleys and the church bells asking, *Were you there*
        when they crucified my lord? After three days alone in the lace-

light, after three days studying a postcard of Krishna bordered by tiny chains of yellow
flowers shooting up and dangling down, I go out at dusk. K drives me beneath

the wings of history, where teenagers slump on the pizza shop steps
        in their coronets. In the fields

yet to be quarried and searched, men in plain clothes ascend
with their children towards a lit house. Tobacco luminous and hip-high.

        So upright I arrive again
        black-skirted with my lemon-sized,
        which I go gladly patterned. And K

sings hymns at the ones holding signs, all red, and they
        draw back and are parted
for us to pass. Even now
I hear the limestone mine's triple horn blows and then, softened by distance,
the inaudible blast.

July 13th, 2013 – July 13th, 2019

IV

H/OURS

On the bulletin board before me hangs a postcard in the style of a postmodern collage. It depicts a classical sculpture of three naked women connected by a veil, joyously embracing; on their pedestal is scrawled graffiti which reads 'Die Zukunft ist weiblich oder gar nicht' (The future is either female or nothing.) The monument is superimposed upon a seascape framed by a broken wall, suggesting war damage, overcome by the ocean reaching to an open blue horizon. In its contrast of muselike idealizations of women and sloppy graffiti, the piece parodies its own slogan; it frames the text of its feminist apocalypse as dissident street work spray-painted under a cloak of darkness, in a burst of stifled laughter.

CATHERINE KELLER

Would there was a plural for *her*. So that I could say: minding the arc, minding her red stalk—and it could mean multiple *hers*, like *theirs*, and also *ours*. H/ours. Minding hours, stalk of red, the contours, the star glass, the blinking rose. Sex is never safe, but neither is time, and nor are flowers.

In their abstract figures, the mammoth, shining kingdom of Family and the abject, bloody queendom of Abortion reign over the American landscape like movie stars. The mood is orchestral, his hand on the small of her back, a painted skyline, feathers, shadows peeled from brick. Shadows licked and stuck to chenille.

Does Abortion do everything Family does only backwards, in heels?

What was first called *purple* was more like our deep red. So blood was purple, the vein and the veil. I thought I could write a story about my country and its bodies sans explication. To destroy explication with purple flowers. And after the destruction, to unfold the hours, to find the pinion-word in an acre of thought.

RUTHIE 1

My grandmother loved Ginger Rogers and Fred Astaire, Esther Williams, aqua alto, sequins and chlorine, American Spirits, the Atlantic Ocean, telemarketers, barrettes. Her TV antennae tipped with foil and every nine minutes the next Newark jet passing over, the next hundred-girl kick-line scissoring across the screen. Didn't we all know that Ruthie had had an abortion, that she had less to do with the kingdom than the queen? *I don't remember how we knew that, but we knew that*, says my mother; *I just remember knowing*. Knowing as a spirit knows, a known tobacco puff, in that five-room Linden bungalow torn down—wires, windows, walls,

all—after her death. Her daughters and her daughters' daughters, laughing, and knowing. Knowing busted sidewalks and azaleas, pink petals thin as rolling papers which we pinned in our hair. Pinned her polyester scarves around each other to make gowns. Obsessed with the picture, but going on the sound. Four brown & white girls running her *shmattehs* up our bodies like flagpoles, what were we but the nation's dance routine?

Ruthie called us the Queen, the Dream, the Brilliant, and the Rose. Before my sister got the Hebrew character for *rose* tattooed on her wrist, the tattooist asked her to double check, so often do people get unfamiliar alphabets permanently wrong. It's true none of us know Hebrew from Adam, although I do know that *dam* means blood. I do remember that we called her Madam, which means we called her *mother, blood.*

Several times I took a tape recorder to her house and didn't mention it. Its red blink tucked between the ashtray and the crosswords. Between the ashes and the going-over jets. Between the door and the veil, with my want—what did I want? Her voice, the obliterating river of it. Grandma, if you & Ben never went to synagogue and never took mommy and Aunt Claire to synagogue and never said the prayers, what has it meant to you to be Jewish? Loudly, on her death cot: *It just feels good, to be Jewish.* And then: *As I said, whatever stage you are in your life, recognize the garbage and get rid of it.*

Primordial 1: Real Voices Talk

It's funny you mention love songs because I loved *love songs, crying my eyes out on the double-decker bus, amateur night on Wednesdays at the Apollo, at the Savoy*

But why were you crying your eyes out

I think of that all the time

My darling, go in the light

As I said, get rid of the garbage out of your life

Come on, I'm going to show you what real voices, real music sounds like

On the 5th Avenue double-decker upstairs

This is whitefish & oil smoke, river to river

I used to ride home with black ink in my hair

And the point is, the whole world flocks to the damn place

A particular shade of blue eyeshadow & my creed

I've got a beautiful tree across the street from me

I wish I was that fucking tree

Let it thunder, let the house crash down

I think I danced in every ballroom in New York

RUTHIE 2

Now go down to the smudges of lumen, go shiveringly down the basement steps. Now go slow, hail her underwear line-hung in the laundry dark. Which she many times told me she'd lent to her *transvestite friends* to go dancing; which are smudges of opal glow unbezeled; which are ships in a fog. Now going slow along the row, the match popped out, it's by the hum of underwearlight I see:

Ruth was born in the same year that Margaret Sanger returned from Europe with a satchel full of diaphragms. At the same time that the American writer Henry James said of the Jews in New York, "These people breed like animals," and described the Lower East Side as the filthiest place on the western continent. By underwearlight

I ask her: Your parents spoke Yiddish? And she says, *Oh are you kidding my mother in fact she was the treasurer and I think eventually the president of—they call a society from—with the women of her, uh, shtetl. Oh they spoke Yiddish, Polish, German*—Did you speak Yiddish? *I don't know*, she says. *I don't think so.*

She was thirteen in the same year the novel *Bad Girl* was published, in which the part of Manhattan where the protagonist goes to get an abortion is pictured as a place where "gossiping uncorsetted Jewesses" hang out on the stoops; in which the villain is a fat Jewess who's had eleven abortions, who wears a giant diamond ring. Such glitter crowns my matriline, although none of the women

from whom I come have ever owned a diamond. However there are the beads like tiny black eyes of birds strung on fine green threads. How Ruthie's mother—Annie Levine born in Kovno, Lithuania, died in New York, New York—stepped off of the ocean with a beaded evening purse and a pile of rags. How when the purse started to disintegrate my mother and her sister, as girls, strung the beads. And one of those strings, I have. Years ago when I referred to the story my mother looked up from her NFL picks and said, *What are you talking about? Those are from a yard sale in New Orleans*. But when I asked more recently they were from the evening purse again.

So keep humming purses and rivers, in the basement of the poem light a match:

By the light of underwear see her rise above the nation, above her pile of rags, with a diamond like a weapon on her hand. With a voice on her back like a wing. Speaking of Annie riding the Atlantic by herself alone at age thirteen I say, It's crazy. *Madness,* Ruthie says, *pure madness. I keep thinking of the word* madness *all the time.*

Primordial 2: Love Songs Talk

So that's how it's going, my angel, that's the thing I can't get out of my mind

109th St. and Madison Avenue, lectures at the YWHA

I hear you've been having sleepless nights

Have you tried listening to love songs

Don't analyze it. Have a shot of booze and lie down and shut up

The miraculous runs shallow and wide

Grandma, this blue cup, or a different cup

Oh please, I learned all of these things by heart

I was discovered in the third grade

With a voice on my back like a wing

Everything else is a distraction

Every night I slap your beautiful face in my mind's eye

My so-called mind

And then I listen to my songs

I realize now that my Perry Como, my John Gary, and Sinatra—that's how they made a lot of money, singing at private parties and occasions

Did you ever get paid to sing

No

RUTHIE 3

On the tape recorder, in the after-glance, Ruthie saying more than once how much my grandfather, her great great love, when he came home from work in the middle of the night like that, when he was kissing her all the way down the block like that, because it was raining, it was one-thirty in the morning, and she had met him at the bus stop with the umbrella, he couldn't get over that altogether, and they were coming down from 5th Avenue, how he couldn't wait to—it was symbolic for him

to slam the door, out of this world. He slammed the door on this world. And that was a symbolic gesture which was essentially her religion. Maybe it's a given that people raised by people who spoke a language limber with *Go*—go break your own head; go break a leg; go drive yourself crazy; go fight City Hall; go peddle your fish elsewhere; go bother the bedbugs; go take a shit for yourself; go

fight heaven—would find it so easy to say, Here is the door and Here is my body and There is yours and There the gold line and Here the borderfire we communicate through, and also to say to those she loved, *Even your crap would be a gift to me*—but never muddy her curtain.

It never occurred to Ruthie that she didn't have a curtain, that she wasn't an important person, marching in the streets. *Marching anywhere that we could*, she said, *always protesting*, it was to be higher than this world, to walk, radiant, and sleep among them, to belong

to the Young Communist League—*I didn't even know it was that*, she says, *but it was*—a critic she felt big and so whatever she came into contact with

> was critical: Critically: *The only contact I had with this*
> *government was to march*
> *against it—Oh, hey, listen,*

you know I'm very fortunate because I'm so damn dead to the world, the only contact was the slam of differentiation, to stalk the borderfire, coming home at night, and Ruthie saying, *He didn't talk too much about personal things in fact you know things that came up here he'd say—to me!—'Don't get personal'*, grinning she says, *I don't know what the hell he thought*, and he knew she was so

damn restless he'd take one
look at her some mornings & say, My God,

we've got to get out of here.

Primordial 3: Sneak Talk

Walking through a door in the tide, walking through a door in the tongue

It is not alone the tenementlight on a pigeon's wing

Or on the ears of a man, a beautiful orphan Jew, coming into the corner drugstore

But the pinioning that grips me

I used to hang out to see if I could get a glimpse of my Ben coming in there

There is no avoiding the erotic

There is no avoiding the trail of holy blanks

Making out between dense river violets

Parts of the city's gold mesh blacked out by leaves

We'd sneak away, we'd sneak to the library

I remember one time we sat on a bench in Central Park—sneakily—in the rain

I don't know why it was always raining in these stories

These stories by the red glare of which I know, and see

Summer dances on the roof of the YWHA, & lectures

Oh my God, the lectures

There is no avoiding the erotic

I had to pass his door on the way to the stairs

What are you trying to do, he says, be the biggest bum on the block

Don't you know I'm crazy about you

Don't you know the difference between one and two

She said, How the hell should I know

She said, Who the hell thinks of marriage

She said, Remember what I told you: while it's raining, wash your hair

RUTHIE 4

The shape it makes, if the men are not included, is a pyramid of seven marks: Ruthie at the top, mother & aunt below, girl cousins & sister & I forming the quadratic base. I have come to see these spiritual lights not as individual rights, not as fireflies drifting to the shoddy melody of lineage, but as sediment, a soluble cluster drawn along. The voiceriver is filled with points of songlight, azalealight, garbagelight, smokelight, but still, years ago at the public library I heard a stranger say, "Where's God? God's so shiny and so we can't see."

I guess I agree. When the seven of us would be planted in the shipped-in sand at the city by the ocean, the mothers were so often weeping laughter, their eyes sealed against the light. Sitting there before the Atlantic off of which their fowl-beheading ancestors had stepped with nits in their hair. Beyond the crackle of tissue packs tucked between their breasts, you couldn't hear a thing because the voiceriver was so tributary-rich and flotsam-blurred. Even now

I see the burning water—
dare I say the burning bush—

when I ask my mother and she says, *We always laughed about it with her*. She says, *My sister and I, we're kind of irreverent people. We're kind of deranged. Your aunt has the same memory; she'll tell you the same thing: We always accused Madam of killing our older brother. If you had a more normal mother she would be more shocked, she would be more how-dare-you, but, that's okay*—the joke was, nobody really wanted a brother, anyway. We're just kind of bobbing along

in a boat called Laughter. Or maybe
it's the boat called Daughter. All we know

is the sound of a lighter scratched, it smashes the atoms of our sleepless nights. Not "individual" but spiritual lights. "Rights" I dislike. Lights get left to themselves on a pigeon's wing. Dear Spirit

of We're-Kind-of-Deranged: Walk with us. As I said, we're in the midst of all this glory and brilliance. It's so shiny and we just—excuse us—

we just can't see. Right at the water's edge,

where the boundless glare begins, we snort, we
foam and fall to our knees.

RUTHIE 5

Sometime in the early decades of the 20th century Ruthie worked as a milliner's assistant. So the river is filled, too, with hatlight, velvetlight, the light of tulle. Her friend Nettie—*one* beauty-*full woman,* Ruthie says—had a little hat store; *she'd look out from behind the partition that we had there, and see who was coming in to buy a hat. She'd take a look she'd say, 'Ruth, I can't stand that bitch, go out and talk to her.' And I'd sell her a hat. That was my beginning,* she says; *that was terrific. After that I worked for Lilly Daché—she was the* top *hat maker in New York, and I wound up trimming her hats.*

Now in an Atlantic reverie, I pull hats from the closet still smelling of tobacco, of Opium perfume. Wearing them, never washing them, I walk through twilit ballrooms where the Jimmy Dorsey orchestra begins to play—*Tangerine, she's all they say with mascara'd eyes, and chapeaux by Daché.*

"Glamor," said Daché, "is what makes a man ask for your telephone number and a woman ask for your dressmaker's name." Eschatology's opposite I say, I say in my country making headway, is undiluted glamor.

So keep humming: *Tangerine with her lips of flame, but her heart belongs to just one, to Tangerine.* It's that citrus greed; it's the undeflectable gaze; a young Jewess with snips of velvet flaming at her feet; the maker of veils. As an air raid warden during the war, Ruthie wore a white hat. *We wore white helmets,* she says, *and walked through the dark streets to make sure*

people had their lights out. We wore white helmets, we wore dark
blossoms, like menstruants we pulled

a curtain across the east, we unraveled the entire city filament
by electric filament, we made it so that planes shouldn't see. We un-

separated the light from the darkness, the earth from the sea.

I guess the joke is that God's so shiny. The joke is that I saw the rivers gray and green to the east and west of the famous island, I drew a figure and colored it gold. I colored gold my mother saying: *I mean, my mother must have said, 'I don't want to be pregnant,' and he must have said something. Because I remember asking her, who did it? And she said Dr. Schecter. It was her doctor, so, she didn't have to go find somebody and that's all I knew.*

Primordial 4: Storm Talk

I went to sleep the other night dreaming of that

I went to sleep the other night, you know, walking

How I loved the walking after a storm

With snow piled up all over the ground

The main thing, it's like, I walked all my life, I walked all over New York

Even to this day if I was in one piece I'd get up and get out that front door

To Eleanor Roosevelt's Camp in Bear Mountain

They announced that anybody who's eighteen and over can go

And I went. Absolutely exquisite business

Every Sunday we put on a play

Once in a while I get haunted by these things

I had the man's role. I had the lowest-toned voice

Went sleigh-riding, as I said

You don't have to report to me, darling

Do whatever you want, I don't give one damn shit

By the lowest-toned voices we ride, my wonderful creature

After a storm with snow all over the ground

Absolutely exquisite business, as I said

[Transcript Postscript]

A: Grandma, did you hear all the thunder and rain?

R: I thought, I thought the house was, part of the house was crashing down! That's what I thought.

JUDITH 1

If you were driving at night you could see them as storm candles, the great purple irises and orange lilies my mother grew at the edge of the woods. Yet more properly they were bright tall genitals of dusk and dawn, furry and structural in the weeds. Hence I grew up eye to eye with fur mouths, talcum powder on their tongues, bush puff poofing out the sides.

In 1965 when my mother was a student at the state university—when she hadn't met my father the Appalachian yet—when the guy she'd been seeing gave her a ride southeast down through green ribs three hours to Philadelphia—he drove her, and he left her there—while staying in a row house which was unfamiliar to her, she wrote a letter to herself which she took home with her over the summer—which she left in the dresser drawer in the room where she slept—which her mother found years later. Although I have never seen the letter in question, I do have a letter of recommendation written on February 19, 1981 by one R.W. Clements:

`To whom it may concern-`

`Ms. Judith Minor has been our contact with the C.E.T.A. program. Ms. Minor is very knowledgeable about the C.E.T.A. program and more improntantly she tries very hard to make it work. It is refreshing to deal with a Federal employee who (1) knows what she is doing (2) willing to do something.`

In my dream these letters are encaustic. Each letter is a bee. Each bee is a woman, writing to herself. Each letter makes a stung gap exactly the shape of itself as it hits the page. It seems to me now that I spent much of my early life following my mother, Ms. Judith Minor, née Berkowitz, through greenhouses in the springs of the years. I think of that when my friend the composer says, "Destroy abortion with flowers and destroy flowers with abortion, that's what your poems should do." And after the destruction—?

I thought I could write less lyrically, but considering my subject I have to mention the greenhouses, sun packed like wool—what else can I do, I can't risk anything but beauty, anything but the opaque, milky tents in which I crawled around on the damp concrete gathering petals—which I coveted for reasons to do with glamor—which she told me to take only if they'd fallen—which I sometimes plucked from the stem.

When Ruthie found the letter my mother had written to herself she said, *Oh my darling, why didn't you tell me, I would have gone with you and protected you.* When my mother relates this story to me she adds, *Just like I said with you.*

JUDITH 2

So there is the letter in a drawer, and there are the flowers burning holes in the long-gone window screens. I see my mother and my grandmother standing in the little hallway where the laundry chute goes down to the basement, where the darkness is strung with underwear. There is the green rick-rack adorning my grandmother's cotton smock; there are the voices stuttering up, heard from another room, and occasionally

something else breaking in, the boundlessness, a wash of salt, the smoketongue, crosswords, so we are caught between surges of light—between voices like nets—so we are standing in the estuary of the soul. When I say, Tell me about your abortion, my mother says something that sounds to me, when I listen back to the recording, like—to destroy

flowers, to destroy orange lilies to drive
down through the bony hills to see them
as storm candles to say
she is very knowledgeable to write to know
what she is doing to be willing
to brush the talcum powder from their gold tongues.

To brush to say I don't even remember, I mean every-
body, everybody knew someone who knew, to
say "purple" to have grits in the morning to write
a letter, to mind the contours and the hours, to laugh
saying I discovered later they charged
more for the white women than the black
women which was totally okay with me to protect
to hold to see eye to eye in the great gold.

To be willing to be lent money, to pay
to be the doctor's mother to take
care to make the grits to show you what real
voices, real music to hold
hands she held your hand while he was
doing it And to say nothing

went wrong I mean they checked on us they didn't
just let us lay there and die in our underwear
with bush puff poofing out the sides to hold
hands to say *shepen naches*, it means Go
gather pleasure—it's a command—and she held,
she held your hand to gather, to gather
flowers, to taste the powder
falling from the great tongues.

[Transcript Postscript]

J: I do that sometimes, I write. But my journals are always so stupid.

A: Mine are, too.

J: No they're not.

A: Even Sylvia Plath's journals get a little bit old—

J: They get old a lot. There's only so much introspection.

A: But what do you think you wrote?

J: I'm so scared, I wonder if my—something like that, I hope everything goes okay, I hope it doesn't go—there's only so much—blah blah, blah, you know.

JUDITH 3

> *What you had in mind has happened; the things you decided on presented themselves and said, 'Here we are!'* —Judith 9:5

Do I know what a story is now? The things you decided on, glittering up through a green wave—there's a car that zooms clear down the back roads linking the front of my mind to the sun. Going slow so there's time to see the little, white Mercedez Benz, to see each color on which the story glides: This guy who in 1965 dated my mother, he had a 190SL with red leather seats and a tan convertible top. For years I've watched it drift

> across the sun bridge like a pulled &
> cleaned & gleaming tooth before it

turns onto an older road that follows dips and hollows. I want to go very slow, I know that today is the greatest day on which the car that I am seeing as a polished, little white tooth slips through trees. Judi(th) drives alone and the leaves are saying, "May the God of our ancestors grant you favor and fulfill your plans." Here we are, the things you decided on,—and do you know the one

about the woman from Bethulia, whose people were dying, their wells guarded by armies of the arrogant king? She went down the mountain and passed through the valley, but first she put fine sandals on her feet, she bathed in coin-clear water when the whole town lay crackling like skins. In this story

she's seventeen, he's Catholic, he feels too guilty and he's started to date someone else. No patrols in this story stop her saying, "To what people do you belong, and where are you coming from, and where are you going?" In this one it's just the beat of leafy eyelashes, nothing about this little drive

is for the exaltation of Jerusalem unless by "Jerusalem" the older story means her *conviction*, a word which points to both punishment and certitude, and dare we—I mean any of us, dare we—be convinced? Do I know what conviction is, how it comes up through the green wave and draws between my mind and the sun a bridge, a god teething marks on the road; how I leaned out once like a green thing while others called, *That's not*

the sun! I wanted to love and be loved by everyone, but I could see
it *was* the sun. Maybe I misunderstand the origins of light & the king

really is God? But dear enemies, dear shifters of the sun: Who can despise
a woman who has such generous thoughts within her? With these thoughts
I've paid for the possible flaw in Judith of Bethulia's certitude, and I'm
not going to unlearn the yearning to humiliate my enemies quite yet. "She
is morally ambiguous," the scholars write. *Listen to me*, says Judith, *your
servant is indeed God-fearing and serves the God of heaven night and day*. When
I ask, Was this

premeditated? She says, *Oh yeah, right*
on the curve of West Whitehall Road I backed up

and boom (and no one, either small
or great, looked in that hour on the work of her hands) *boom, boom*
back and forth
into the tree. She says, *The tree's still there.*

JUDITH 4

> *Judith said, 'I will gladly drink, my lord, because today is the greatest day in my whole life.'* —Judith 12:18

In the old story she leaves the general's tent, and who isn't cheering when she hands Holofernes's bloody head to her maid, who sticks it in their food sack for the amble home? In my story she just drives back, parks the car, gives him the keys, and says, *My Lord, the car's in the parking lot.* And the leaves whisper, Really, what a gift, her foot on the gas, the boom which illuminates.

So the little, white Mercedez Benz was completely crunched. And the tree? We hurry down to see the white oak the summer I'm thirty-one. It's eighty feet tall with a scar running up its body and so many leaves scalloped like ten thousand packets of bright green rick rack for somebody's giant cotton smock to sew. And when I ask

whether she was worried about hurting
herself she says, *Well, I was going*

very slow.

ABIGAIL 1

So. Is there a gold line, rough, like a hem, to one side of which I stand? Is there a doorway, the curtain we communicate through, and the door, and the immolating slam? If it is true, as is so often suggested, that pregnancy, in the words of the essayist Eula Biss, "Confound[s]...the distinction between self and nonself," is it also true that the desire not to be pregnant represents an unwillingness to blur that distinction? How intricately

one smokes on a balcony in the rain, one marches in the streets, intricately
            images of women marking the borderfire slink in
and out of the shadows of my love cloud: there's Ruth in her cotton smock,

sitting in her chair. On the screen, fire fountains shot from an Olympic-sized pool and Esther Williams diving, a silver needle smiling into the glass. Sometimes even in love Ruthie shouting, *Oh enough with your dippy face!* and clicking it off.

A quarter of a century later my sister saying, *Family—family. We were the family where the grandma and the moms made the kids go fart near other people on the beach so they'd leave.* Beneath Venus star of morning, star of evening, facing the Atlantic filled with its tonnage and debris: Go fart near them, so they'll leave. So we

            were like noisy stars in the sky, and sand in the sea. And all those who were not brought forth never had a chance to nurse strips of button candy dot by dot, to peel disks of paper from their tongues; they never played dress-up in the rental balcony's jade dusk, where muted images of some far-off desert filled with men & guns were doubled, opal-washed, in the sliding door's glass. Having seen, having been a star, writing now far from the city and the sand, it's as the Brilliant that I've donned my feathered abortion hat, in which to have my American dreams:

As in the sensational 1871 Trunk Mystery, abortion providers in the city papers were usually described as foreign, and big-nosed. Their patients as feeble and blonde. Once at a midtown deli I ordered whitefish and my blonde lover got American cheese. I glanced into the mirror and saw a gold gleam in my mouth and a rag on my head. I was his abortionist and he was a beautiful dead woman locked in a trunk. We were together, laughing by the sea. It's possible I was wearing my A(merica)n hat, and having an a(bortio)n dream. When I asked for mine toasted, the guy working there said, “Mami, we don’t toast.” Evidently it’s poor form in New York bagel etiquette to toast. I didn’t know that, as I grew up in Pennsylvania eating Miracle Whip on matzah.

Primordial 5: Grand/Daughter Talk

Once in the lead blur of a hurricane's edge, I saw the ocean's scrap metal mouths

I saw a ton of lilies white in the water's booming hair

I looked up and saw a woman on a balcony lean out with a cigarette in her hand

I was a little puff and she was a red root deep in the air

I was a brown beach stone and she was a white t-shirt on the moon

We hold these (women) to be self-(interested)

Life begins when you've lent your beloved friends your underwear

You're nobody till somebody loves you, you're nobody till somebody cares

Was she adding a rivet to the distinction between self and nonself

I was cigarette holes the size of a pencil eraser burnt into her sheets

So goddamn beautiful she was crying her eyes out

As I said, exquisite business, canescent in the dark

[Transcript Postscript]

R: *Oh you sound so sweet and pure—you don't take any crap from anybody, you hear?*

A: *Grandma, no one wants to give me any crap.*

R: *Darling, whoever doesn't want to give you any crap doesn't know what they're missing.*

RUTHIE/JUDITH

Ruthie giving birth & it was snowing. *Twenty-six inches of snow in New York,* she says, *the maternity hospital was in the Bronx. I was in a room with five women; we laughed ourselves sick giving birth with nits in our hair. Afterwards the doctor and me were going down in the elevator I said, Doctor I need a cigarette, he said,*

Ruthie you know you can't be smoking in here; I said, Please, if you don't give me a cigarette I'm gonna die—please, in the drift down between greased cables, her muscular sex gravity-hushed, her city out there in deep snow & *Oh,*

> *he gave me a cigarette.* (Puff,
> puff.) *Dr. Schecter.*

Underneath the talk there are the sounds of remedy stuttering up, in my smoketongue I fly over the rivers, I watch ash fall like black pollen on the snow. And Dr. Schecter, whoever the hell you are, and my mother's doctor, and his mother, I greet you

> in the after-glance, so enrobed

I meet you on the disobedient's path. Hale in underwearlight I pass through the long-stemmed velvet of the birthing night. And reader, I give this blessing for you, my reader, pin back your ears:

We laughed against the world we

were dead to it & hauling

ourselves dripping from the flame

all of these things by heart by heart we knew

the way we flew the borders we shit for ourselves

we swam the voice river with nits

in our hair we unseparated the dark

from the light & laughed ourselves brilliant

between the blackout trumpets & the match

just flicked, we laughed

ourselves tender, laughed ourselves sick.

NOTES & ACKNOWLEDGEMENTS

Many thanks to those who have previously published, adapted, or presented some of these poems: A version of "Real Words for Inside" was published in 2018 as a chapbook by Gap Riot Press, edited by Kate Siklosi and Dani Spinosa. A version of "H/ours" was published under a different title in *apt*, edited by Carissa Halston and Randolph Pfaff. "Once in a Black Silk Gown: A Film Noir" is featured in an episode of Arts & Letters, a radio program hosted by J. Bradley Minnick of the University of Arkansas. Excerpts from "Once…" also appear in a film adaptation by the musician Kevin Sims, first presented at the Bremen Town Ballroom in Millheim, Pennsylvania as part of the Open Music Series.

In writing this book I have grappled with and often rejected the notion that our bodies are wholly individual and autonomous. I wrote these poems alone in a room, but I was never unaccompanied. I am indebted to activists, ancestors, enemies, and poets; to politicians, neighbors, dreams, and strangers; as well as to the following sources, cradles, sparks, sparring partners, and nocking points:

Abortion in the American Imagination ("how antiabortion rhetoric was used to delineate the contours of the ideal American citizen" / Weingarten, 2014); *When Abortion was a Crime* ("Our understanding of what punishment is needs to be refined and redefined, particularly in cases of women who violate sexual norms" / Reagan, 1998); *No Future* ("the illusion of the future as suture" / Edelman, 2004); *Contraception and Abortion in 19th-Century America* ("'Its application is easy and accomplished in a moment without the aid of a light'"/ Brodie, 1994); *Breeding Contempt* ("to lay bare our ongoing compulsion to locate the source of complex problems within certain citizens' testicles and ovaries" / Largent, 2011); *Stardust Lost* ("The sounds of laughter and desire serve as a powerful counterpoint to the sighs of resignation" / Kanfer, 2006); *Blood, Bread, and Roses* ("adornment itself is speech" / Grahn, 1994); *Eve's Herbs* ("'boil willow bark down and drink it continually with honey'" / Riddle, 1999); *Back Rooms* ("'It sounds really simple now, but it was not simple'" / eds. Messer & May, 1988); *Reproductive Acts* ("all reproductive choices are grossly political" / Latimer, 2013); *Killing the Black Body* ("surely the inheritability of race plays some role in the degree of importance whites invest in genetic ties with their children" / Roberts, 1998); *The Queen of America Goes to Washington City* ("the logic by which the pregnant woman sutures femininity, nature, and nation" / Berlant, 1997); *Abortion, Choice, and Contemporary Fiction* ("Consciousness itself implies loss" / Wilt, 1990); *Black and Blur* ("something keeps on coming out of nowhere" / Moten, 2017); *In the Pines* ("This is your defect / it might as well be / a diamond" / Notley, 2007); *Angels in America: A Gay Fantasia on National Themes* ("That was heaven, Roy" / Kushner, 1993).

Particular and essential to "Once in a Black Silk Gown: A Film Noir":

Rereading Sex ("Close to the bright lights of minstrelsy the sporting press came into being"; "Attacks emphasized Restell's wealth and audacious manner"; "This was a world in which only men mattered" / Horowitz, 2003); "Advertising Abortion During the 1830s and 1840s" ("One observer said the abortion advertisements' code words were known to 'every schoolgirl' in New York" / Orlasky, 1986); *Jump Jim Crow* ("'Don't you hear de banjo tum, tum, tum!'" / Lhamon, 2003); *Gotham Unbound* ("Filling in land under water eventually burgeoned into a fixation for the English colonists" / Steinberg, 2015); *Mannahatta* ("It's not a stretch to say that red columbines grew in Harlem" / Sanderson, 2013); *Madame Restell: An Account of Her Life and Horrible Practices* ("The subject is too delicate for explanation" / anonymous, 1847); *Wonderful trial of Caroline Lohman, alias Restell: with speeches of counsel, charge of court, and verdict of jury: reported in full for the National Police Gazette* (anonymous, 1847); *The Wickedest Woman in New York* (Browder, 1988); *Scandalous Lady* (Keller, 1981). This cycle is especially indebted to A. Cheree Carlson's *The Crimes of Womanhood* (2008): "[at times] the physical body of Lohman was directly affected by the symbolic body of Restell"; "Restell had had enough of rhetoric and withdrew from the fight." Thanks also to The Patricia D. Klingenstein Library at the New-York Historical Society for access to two tracts by anonymous writers: *The Restell Suicide: Her Secret Life* (1890) and *Trial of Madame Restell, Alias Ann Lohman* ("certain acts have certain consequences" / 1841). Where I have for brevity's sake in a few cases conflated minor figures and events, the books by Horowitz and Carlson will serve readers in search of a straight record. The floral radiograph mentioned in "Footage" refers to an x-ray image by Merrill Raikes.

Briefly I would like to mention that although Lohman was one of the most visible (and elite) abortion providers of her day, she was certainly not the only one. Countless midwives, community doctors, and herbalists served the reproductive needs of rural and urban communities. Over the decades, many forces contributed to the persecution and disappearance of these health care providers and the folkways they followed. The rise of the American Medical Association; the emergence of gynecology as a legitimate and lucrative area of practice for white male doctors; and increasingly punitive laws regarding abortion all contributed to the ousting of folk practitioners, the vast majority of whom were women, black, and/or immigrants. This is not to say that the codification of medical training and provision was motivated only by capitalism and its attendant forces, but to acknowledge, then as now, that issues other than public health were at play. Many of the secondary sources listed above helped me to understand the enormous changes in medical, legal, economic, and social systems of the U.S. that Lohman and others navigated throughout the nineteenth century.

Places where there are humor and insouciance in these poems mark moments of triumph over—or at least moments of succeeding at living with—first- and secondhand experiences of the trauma, terror, and sorrow inflicted by those who would force pregnable people to actualize the fantasies of others. Yet this work was ultimately propelled by experiences of pleasure, power, and love. I am grateful to everyone who talked, theorized, wept, and laughed with me about this book and its subjects over many years. In particular, I thank the West St. Schoolhouse residency crew, Melissa Madera and The Abortion Diary Podcast, and Peg Johnston and everyone at Abortion Conversation Projects for their friendship and insights. Thanks also to all who've shared their reproductive stories with me, sometimes off the cuff and on the fly, especially Genny Uhl and those who've taken part in various makeshift rural actions and conversations.

For intelligent and loving attention to large portions of this work, often in earliest and untamed forms, I thank MRB Chelko, Sara DiCaglio, Cynthia Clem, Lee Peterson, and Evan McGarvey. Also teachers who made straight (and winding, and wondrous) the way: Robin Becker, Kevin Quashie, Daniel Horowitz, Rip Lhamon, Jennifer Anne Tucker, Annie-hannah E. Mancini, and Hilton Als. Thanks to Julia Spicher Kasdorf for opening the door and trespassing in the name of poetry.

I am centrally grateful to my mother, Judith Berkowitz Minor, for sharing her voice and her indomitable style with me. And to my sister, Rebecca Paige Minor, for countless conversations about courage and self-compassion. I dedicate "Real Words for Inside" to the memory of my father, Ellsworth Dale Minor, Jr.

For time and space in which to make these poems, I thank the Ora Lerman Charitable Trust, The Rensing Center, and Liora O'Donnell Goldensher, who gave me a room from which I could walk to Roosevelt Island and hot soup at night. Thanks also to the C.D. Wright Women Writers Conference for recognizing an earlier version of "H/ours" with a Nan Snow Emerging Writer Award. I am gladly indebted to Erin Lynch for insightful and heartfelt editing; to Sandra Rosales and Scott Dennison for beautiful design work; to Laia Abril for her luminous cover photograph; and to Thomas Renjilian and everyone else at Ricochet Editions for taking such good care.

I could not have written this book without Julie Swarstad Johnson, beloved correspondent, who read every page and then some. Nor could I have written it without Kevin Sims, champion of elsewhere and otherwise.

For those readers interested in learning more about progressive abortion care and reproductive justice, I recommend the Abortion Care Network (ACN), Inroads, Abortion Conversation Projects, Women on Waves, Socorristas en Red, National Advocates for Pregnant Women, Sister Song, and *Radical Reproductive Justice* (2017, The Feminist Press). Independent providers such as those with membership in the ACN provide 60% of all abortions in the U.S. All-Options runs a talk-line for those who are thinking through any and all experiences with pregnancy, parenting, abortion, infertility, and adoption, 1-888-493-0092. Resources for finding a clinic, finding and using abortion pills safely, and more are at ShareSafeAbortion.Info.

Finally, my deepest thanks and affection to abortion care providers everywhere. Selah.

Abby Minor lives in the ridges and valleys of central Pennsylvania, where she works on poems, essays, quilts, and projects exploring reproductive politics. Granddaughter of Appalachian tinkerers and Yiddish-speaking New Yorkers, she teaches poetry in her region's low-income nursing homes and has worked as a seamstress, server, university writing instructor, studio assistant, and roadie. In 2018 she was awarded Bitch Media's Writing Fellowship in Sexual Politics. She serves on the board of Abortion Conversation Projects; is author of the chapbooks *Real Words for Inside* (Gap Riot Press) and *Plant Light, Dress Light* (dancing girl press); and directs an arts education nonprofit called Ridgelines Language Arts.

author photo: Jennifer Anne Tucker